Amazing Animals
Wolves

Angela Royston

W

WEIGL PUBLISHERS INC.

Published by Weigl Publishers Inc.
350 5th Avenue, Suite 3304, PMB 6G
New York, NY 10118-0069

Amazing Animals series ©2010
WEIGL PUBLISHERS INC. www.weigl.com
All rights reserved. No part of this
publication may be reproduced, stored
in a retrieval system, or transmitted in
any form or by any means, electronic,
mechanical, photocopying, recording,
or otherwise, without the prior written
permission of the publisher.

Library of Congress Cataloging-in-
Publication Data

Library of Congress Cataloging-in-
Publication Data available upon request.
Fax 1-866-44-WEIGL for the attention of
the Publishing Records department.

ISBN 978-1-60596-156-9 (hard cover)
ISBN 978-1-60596-157-6 (soft cover)

Editor
Heather Kissock
Design and Layout
Terry Paulhus, Kathryn Livingstone

Photograph Credits
Every reasonable effort has been
made to trace ownership and to obtain
permission to reprint copyright material.
The publishers would be pleased to have
any errors or omissions brought to their
attention so that they may be corrected
in subsequent printings.

Weigl acknowledges Getty Images as its
primary image supplier for this title.

Printed in China
1 2 3 4 5 6 7 8 9 0 13 12 11 10 09

About This Book

This book tells you all about
wolves. Find out where they live
and what they eat. Discover how
you can help to protect them. You
can also read about them in myths
and legends from around
the world.

Words in **bold** are explained in the
Words to Know section at the back
of the book.

Useful Websites

Addresses in this book
take you to the home
pages of websites that
have information
about wolves.

All of the Internet URLs given in
the book were valid at the time
of publication. However, due to
the dynamic nature of the Internet,
some addresses may have changed,
or sites may have ceased to exist
since publication. While the author
and publisher regret any
inconvenience this may cause
readers, no responsibility for any
such changes can be accepted by
either the author or the publisher.

Contents

Meet the Wolf

A wolf is an animal with sharp teeth and a thick fur coat. Wolves belong to the same family of animals as pet dogs. Wolves are **predators**, which means they hunt other animals for food.

▼ A wolf can travel many miles at a fast pace.

Most wolves live in family groups. They like to roam in natural areas, far away from people. People may hear a wolf **howling** in the distance, but they will probably never see one.

Useful Websites

www.boomerwolf.com

Visit this website for fun games and useful information.

Wolf Relatives

These animals all belong to the dog family.

- gray wolves
- red wolves
- coyotes
- jackals
- huskies
- all other pet dogs

▲ Wolves may look like pet dogs, but they behave very differently and do not make good pets.

Expert Hunters

A wolf's strong, quick body helps it chase and catch other animals. A wolf can run at high speed through thick forests and across snowy ground. A wolf's eyes, ears, and nose help it track down **prey**. A wolf kills animals with its long, sharp teeth.

The Amazing Wolf

- A wolf can hear sounds from as far away as 6 to 10 miles (10 to 16 kilometers).

- A wolf can run for about 22 miles (35 km) without stopping to rest.

- A wolf can smell other animals that are more than 1 mile (1.6 km) away.

A wolf's keen eyesight is useful for spotting other animals.

Large ears pick up even the quietest sounds.

A wolf's thick fur keeps the animal warm in the winter.

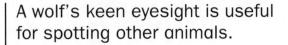

A wolf's sharp teeth are used for tearing meat.

An excellent sense of smell helps a wolf find food.

A wolf can run across snow without sinking on its large, broad feet.

A wolf has long, powerful legs.

Where Do Wolves Live?

Most wolves live in cold places far to the north. A wolf's home might be a huge forest or an isolated valley. Some wolves live in places where it is too cold for trees to grow. Here, the land is covered with snow for most of the year.

▼ Grizzly bears live in many of the same areas as wolves.

Wolves were once found in many countries of the world. Today, only a few wolves live in warmer countries. Such countries include Mexico, Greece, Spain, and India.

Useful Websites

www.nationalgeographic.com/geoguide/wolves

Visit this website to learn about wolves and their neighbors.

▲ Most wolves make their homes in large, forested areas.

Living with Wolves

There are many different kinds of animals that live in the same places as wolves.

- Arctic hares
- bears
- beavers
- caribou
- cougars
- coyotes
- deer
- moose
- musk oxen

What Do Wolves Eat?

Wolves need to eat meat to stay alive. They like to hunt large animals, such as deer, moose, and caribou. When food is hard to find, wolves eat any kind of animal they can catch. A small meal for a wolf might be a mouse, a rabbit, or a beaver.

Several wolves will work together to chase and kill large prey. They sniff out an animal and sneak up on it. Then, all the wolves attack at once. The oldest wolves eat first.

▶ A wolf has four very long teeth at the front of its mouth. These teeth are used to grab and tear meat.

What a Meal!

- A wolf can eat 13 pounds (5 kilograms) of meat in one meal. This is the same as eating three whole chickens, eight large hamburgers, and 16 sausages!

▲ A wolf on its own can easily catch a small animal, such as an Arctic hare.

Family Life

Most wolves live in a group called a **pack**. There are usually between 5 and 12 wolves in a pack. They hunt together over a large area of land. This land is called their **territory**.

▼ Wolves watch out for danger. If other wolves come near, the pack chases them away.

A male wolf and a female wolf are in charge of the pack. The other wolves are their babies, or pups. Many pups stay with the pack once they have grown up.

Useful Websites

www.wolf.org

Visit this website to see photographs and film clips of wolves.

Wolf Talk

- When wolves wake up, they howl to say "hello" to each other.

- Wolves howl to tell other members of the pack where they are.

- A loud howl warns wolves that are not in the pack to stay away.

Growing Up

A mother wolf makes a **den** for her babies, or pups. The den might be under the ground, in a cave, or inside a hollow log. About six pups are born in a **litter**. At first, the tiny pups just sleep and feed on milk from their mother.

Soon, the pups begin to play together and learn how to hunt. All the wolves in the pack help to look after and feed the growing pups.

▼ Pups stay in the den until they are strong enough to explore outside.

14

▲ A mother teaches her pups how to smell trails made by other animals.

Comparing Weights

◼ Human ◼ Wolf

At birth	8 pounds (3.6 kg) 1 pound (0.4 kg)
At 8 weeks	10 pounds (4.5 kg) 15 pounds (6.8 kg)
Adult male	168 pounds (76.3 kg) 130 pounds (59 kg)

0   25   50   75   100   125   150   175 pounds

Enemies

Wolves often fight with other wolves. Sometimes a wandering wolf strays into the territory, or land, of another pack. The pack will attack the stranger and chase it away.

Wolves in the same pack fight each other, too. Two wolves may fight to find out which is stronger. Other wolves struggle for a share of the food.

▶ Wolves bare their teeth to scare other wolves away.

◀ If a cougar comes across a wolf, it will usually climb a tree for safety.

Animal Thieves

Some of these animals may try to steal food from wolves.

- bears
- cougars
- coyotes
- magpies
- ravens

Under Threat

People are the biggest danger to wolves. Wolves have trouble finding food when people build farms and houses in the places where wolves live. Many people want to protect wolves, but others are afraid of them. Farmers sometimes shoot wolves because they fear a hungry wolf may kill cattle and sheep.

▼ Sometimes, wolves are captured and released into new areas for their safety.

Groups of people are trying to save wolves. They catch the animals and take them to new forests. There is plenty of food in these areas.

Useful Websites

www.nwf.org/wolves

Find out how you can help protect wolves by visiting this website.

▲ Most wolves try to keep away from people. They stay in areas that are mainly wilderness.

What Do You Think?

Should people take wolves back to safe forests where these animals once roamed?

Myths and Legends

Since the earliest times, people around the world have told stories about wolves.

Fairy Tales

Fairy tales show wolves as wicked, greedy animals. In the story *Little Red Riding Hood*, a wolf gobbles up Little Red Riding Hood's grandmother. In *The Three Little Pigs*, a wolf tries to eat three piglets.

▼ In stories such as *Little Red Riding Hood*, wolves prey on helpless humans.

Useful Websites

www.wolfweb.com

Visit this website to find games and wolf tales.

Wolf Brother

The American Indian Pawnee thought that wolves were their brothers. In some stories, the wolf teaches them to hunt **bison**. In other stories, the wolf teaches them to share their food with one another.

Mistakes about Wolves

People say many things about wolves that are not true.

- Wolves do not howl at the Moon.

- Healthy wolves do not attack humans.

- Wolves are not greedy.

◀ In some stories, wolves howl at the full Moon. Wolves in nature do not howl at the Moon.

Quiz

1. Why do wolves howl?
   (*a*) **to frighten people** (*b*) **to catch food**
   (*c*) **to keep in touch with each other**

2. Which of these animals may attack wolves?
   (*a*) **crocodiles** (*b*) **bears** (*c*) **deer**

3. What do newborn wolf pups feed on?
   (*a*) **milk** (*b*) **fruit** (*c*) **meat**

4. Where do most wolves live?
   (*a*) **in hot places** (*b*) **in cold places**
   (*c*) **in rainy places**

5. What is a family group of wolves called?
   (*a*) **a territory** (*b*) **a pack** (*c*) **a flock**

Answers:
1. (c) Wolves howl to keep in touch with each other.
2. (b) Only bears may attack wolves.
3. (a) Newborn wolf pups feed on milk.
4. (b) Most wolves live in cold places.
5. (b) A family group of wolves is called a pack.

Find out More

To find out more about wolves, visit the websites in this book. You can also write to these organizations.

International Wolf Center
1396 Highway 169
Ely, MN 55731-8129

North American Wolf Society
P.O. Box 82950
Fairbanks, AK 99708

The Wolf Fund
P.O. Box 471
Moose, WY 83012

Wolf Haven International
3111 Offut Lake Road
Tenino, WA 98589

Words to Know

bison
a wild ox that lives in North America
America

den
an animal's home, where it may find
shelter or look after its babies

howling
the sound wolves make to communicate

litter
the group of pups born to a mother wolf

pack
a family group of wolves

predators
animals that hunt other animals
for food

prey
an animal that is hunted for food

territory
the land on which a pack of wolves
lives and hunts

Index